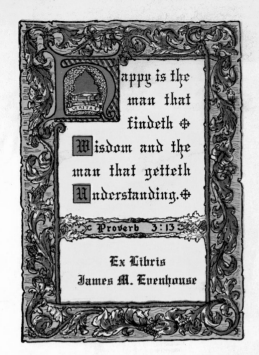

appy is the man that findeth ✦ **W**isdom and the man that getteth **U**nderstanding. ✦

◁ Proverb 3:13 ▷

Ex Libris
James M. Evenhouse

# THE LORD'S PRAYER

# THE LORD'S PRAYER

BY

## HENRY BAST

THE CHURCH PRESS
1957
GRAND RAPIDS, MICHIGAN

The author, the Rev. Henry Bast, is the minister of *Temple Time*, a radio broadcast of the Reformed Church in America. This broadcast is heard throughout America and broadcasted overseas in three languages—Japanese, Chinese and Tamil in India.

Dr. Bast has served successful pastorates in Grand Rapids, Michigan and is at present Lector in the Department of Practical Theology at Western Theological Seminary, Holland, Michigan.

Last year Dr. Bast was given an honorary degree, doctor of divinity, from his alma mater, Hope College, in recognition of his leadership and ability.

This edition of sermons is typical of the preaching of Dr. Bast. Originally these messages were broadcasted over *Temple Time* and have now been revised for book publication. The clear-cut language, the direct illustrations and the deep-rooted Biblical messages are useful to laymen and preachers who desire a better insight into The Lord's Prayer.

# FOREWORD

Prayer is probably the most talked about and least used of all Christian experiences. Some will preach, more will give, many will work, but who will pray? Who will seek that better part which Mary was wise enough to choose? Who will storm the gates of heaven, that God's power may save and transform the hearts of men here on earth?

Every faithful disciple of our Lord Jesus Christ knows something about prayer. Origen describes the Christian life as one continuous prayer. Every earnest disciple, eager to know more about prayer, turns his face to heaven and asks, "Lord, teach me to pray." Our Saviour, whose life was one of continuous praying, was ever urging His disciples to give more time and effort to this exercise. "Ask and it shall be given you, seek and ye shall find, knock and it shall be opened unto you," He promised. Facing a crisis that was sure to test them to the utmost He warned, "Watch and pray, lest ye enter into temptation." Our Lord is waiting to teach us how to pray today through His Word and Spirit.

Dr. Henry Bast, a true writer instructed in the kingdom of God, here brings forth things new and old on the theme of Prayer. A study of this book will bring instruction and strength to our souls.

LOUIS H. BENES,
Editor - *The Church Herald*

# CONTENTS

# CHAPTER I

# WHY SHOULD WE PRAY?

*"After this manner therefore pray ye . . ."*
(MATTHEW 6:9)

This series of meditations is based on the prayer Jesus taught His disciples which we commonly call the Lord's Prayer. There is always need for instruction in prayer but we particularly need it in a day like ours when more and more people are turning to religion. That there is a new interest in religion today is evident on every hand and with this return to religion, there is also a new interest in prayer.

It is equally evident, however, that with a new emphasis on the importance of prayer, many are woefully ignorant of the true meaning of prayer. Many people are now praying who have zeal but no knowledge. Recently the newspapers across the country carried the sensational story of a woman in Washington who believed that she could raise the dead by prayer. When her roommate died, she preserved the body in her apartment for eighteen months and tried through prayer to restore her to life. When the body was finally discovered in her apartment she said, "I was praying constantly, praying every day. Tuesday night I stayed up and prayed all night."

Even though this is an extreme case, there are people who take incidents like that and blame the failure on prayer. They use such incidents as an argument against the validity of prayer. Perhaps you have failed to obtain something you prayed for, and because of that failure you say that you have lost your faith in prayer. Such failures, however, should not be used to attack the validity of prayer; they only betray our ignorance about prayer.

Surely there is enough positive evidence in the Scripture and in Christian history and in our own age to establish the validity of prayer. Prayer is a mighty force. Tennyson was right when he said, "More things are wrought by prayer than this world dreams of." These words from Tennyson are in a speech of good King Arthur and you may recall how the great king went on to say,

> *Wherefore let thy voice*
> *Rise like a fountain for me night and day.*
> *For what are men better than sheep or goats*
> *That nourish a blind life within the brain,*
> *If, knowing God, they lift not hands of prayer*
> *Both for themselves and those who call them friend?*
> *For so the whole earth is, every way,*
> *Bound by gold chains, about the feet of God.*

Most of our failures in prayer are due to our lack of knowledge about prayer. For understanding we must take our questions about prayer to Jesus Christ, the world's greatest example, and the world's greatest teacher on prayer.

The first question about prayer we would ask is, "Why should we pray?" In the course of this study we will see that this question is answered for us, not only in the teachings of Jesus, but everywhere in the Bible. In the Word of God we find three reasons why prayer is necessary.

The first is gratitude. Prayer is a duty we owe to God. It is the major expression of the thankfulness we owe to Him for all His blessings toward us. In Luke's account of the ministry of Jesus we read that one day ten lepers came to Him in their pathetic condition, begging Him to consider their plight. In His goodness and mercy Jesus healed all ten lepers. Some time later one of the ten came back to thank Christ for His healing power and mercy. In astonishment, Jesus looked at the one man who had come back and said, "Were not the ten cleansed, but where are the nine?" He then asked, "Were there none found that returned to give glory to God, save this stranger" (Luke 17:17, 18, ASV)? Have you ever thought of prayer in the light of God's goodness to you? Jesus teaches that all men should give thanks to God for the blessings that He has bestowed upon them. Whatever you have, even life itself, is given you by God Almighty. Every good and perfect gift comes from God, who freely disposes His blessings upon all men.

Though all men should give thanks to God, those who have been redeemed by His grace ought most of all to come to Him in gratitude. See how often in Scripture God's redeemed children are exhorted to thank Him for their salvation. The 107th Psalm is typical of many. "O, give thanks unto the Lord, for he is good: for his mercy endureth for ever. Let the redeemed of the Lord say so, whom he hath redeemed from the hand of the enemy" (1, 2). Paul writes to the Thessalonians: "Pray without ceasing. In every thing give thanks: for this is the will of God in Christ Jesus concerning you" (I Thess. 5:17, 18). To the Philippians he writes, "In nothing be anxious; but in everything by prayer and supplication with thanksgiving let your requests be made known unto God" (4:6, ASV). Paul writes to the Colossians, "And whatsoever ye do, in word or in deed, do all in the name of the Lord Jesus, giving thanks to God the Father through him" (3:17, ASV); "Continue stedfastly in prayer, watching therein with thanksgiving" (4:2, ASV). When we observe the emphasis there is in the Bible on prayer as thanksgiving, we look at the whole question of prayer, not as a means of seeking more, but as an opportunity to give thanks for what we have. God is our heavenly Father who has already pardoned our sins by grace and made us His children. He anticipates our every need for body and soul. Because God is good we must give thanks.

Not long ago I went to visit one of the members of our church who was ready to leave the hospital after surgery. The patient I was visiting told me that the finest testimony she heard all the

time she was in the hospital was from the colored maid who came
to clean her room. This Negro woman spoke to her of the goodness of God and said that she thanked God for everything. After
she had named some of the things in our modern life she was
thankful for, she said, "It hurts me when they say that man did
all this." Do you love God so much and are you so aware of
your dependence on Him and are you so conscious of His goodness and mercy that you are hurt when men ignore or deny God?
As children of God, the first reason why we must pray is to
express thanks to God for what He has already done. We see
therefore that our thinking about prayer does not begin in
asking God to do something more, but in thanking Him for
what He has already done.

The second reason why prayer is necessary is that it is the
appointed means of obtaining the blessing God has ordained
for us. There are some who ask, "Why pray? If God knows
what we need, why is it necessary for us to ask Him?" Jesus
anticipates this objection. When He commands us to pray, He
says, "For your Father knoweth what things ye have need of, before
ye ask him" (Matt. 6:8). Here Jesus teaches that we must pray in
spite of the fact that God knows what we need before we ask
Him. This teaches us what prayer does not do. We are not to
pray to God as if He is ignorant and needs to be informed of
our wants, neither are we to argue with God as if He needs to
be persuaded to help us. We must pray to God as our Father
who knows all our needs and is willing and able to help us.
Prayer is the means by which we are to obtain the blessings that
God intends to give us.

There are others who do not pray because they have a kind
of fatalistic attitude toward life. We find this attitude in a popular
song, "Whatever will be, will be." Such people say, "All things
will happen anyway, so what difference does it make if we pray
or do not pray." If this is your objection to prayer, then let me
remind you that we do not speak like that in other matters. Your
house is probably equipped to use electricity. The power lines

are connected to the house and all the fixtures are installed. Because this work is completed the men working for the power company say, "They have power." But your home remains dark until you turn on the switch. The house is wired for electricity, the meter is in, the power is there, but the light does not go on until you turn the switch.

In the same way God has appointed prayer as the means by which we are to obtain all His blessings. He has so ordered life that these blessings are given only to those who earnestly seek them. This is one of the primary reasons why we must pray. The Bible teaches us that God will give us all things necessary for soul and body if we ask Him. This is what the Word of God says, "Ask and it shall be given, seek and ye shall find, knock and it shall be opened unto you." "The Lord is nigh unto all them that call upon him in truth." "Draw nigh to God and he will draw nigh to you." "The Lord is found of them who seek him with all their heart." When we observe this teaching of the Word of God we see how it is wrong to neglect prayer. It is costly not to pray, for if we do not pray we cut ourselves off from the blessings that God has promised us. This is well expressed by Richard Trench in one of the most beautiful sonnets on prayer in the English language.

> *Lord, what a change within us one short hour*
> *Spent in Thy presence will prevail to make!*
> *What heavy burdens from our bosoms take,*
> *What parched grounds refresh as with a shower!*
> *We kneel and all around us seem to lower;*
> *We rise, and all, the distant and the near,*
> *Stands forth in sunny outline brave and clear;*
> *We kneel, how weak! we rise, how full of power!*

The third reason we must pray is because it strengthens our faith. Prayer is necessary not only because it is the means by which God supplies all our needs but because the act of praying strengthens us. Praying increases our faith. It builds up hope in the promises of God. It releases our minds from the cares of this world and fixes mind and heart on God and heaven. This is not to speak of a mere psychological value of prayer. There are many in our day who have lost this faith in an omnipotent, personal God, who still retain the practice of prayer because they say it does them good to pray. Such writers speak of the psychological or reflexive value of prayer. It is true that there is such value in praying, but it is true only because there is Someone who is listening. Because God listens to us it does us good to pray. Remind yourself when you pray that you are talking to your Father in heaven and that He has promised to listen to you, and you will find the very act of praying a strong defense against temptation and sin. You will also discover the wonderful comfort and benefit that come to you as you pour out your soul to God in prayer. Look to God, cry to Him. He invites you to cast your burdens and all your troubles upon Him. Prayer is an effective means of restoring strength and hope in our hearts because God hears us when we pray.

> *Why, therefore, should we do ourselves this wrong,*
> *Or others, that we are not always strong,*
> *That we are ever overborne with care,*
> *That we should ever weak or heartless be,*
> *Anxious or troubled, when with us is prayer,*
> *And joy and strength and courage are with Thee!*

Having given three basic reasons why we should pray, let us now see the importance of praying in the right manner. When Jesus said, "After this manner therefore pray ye," He was teaching us how to pray because there are some prayers God does not hear. Jesus Himself said that God did not hear the prayers of the Pharisees because they were hypocrites. He also said that God does not hear the vain repetitions of the Gentiles. If such prayers are not heard, you see how important it is that we should pray in the right manner. What kind of prayer does God hear? We find as we study the New Testament that there are three marks of true prayer.

The first is that we must call upon God from the heart. The Pharisees were not heard because they were insincere. Their prayers never reached the throne of grace. We should observe also the teaching of the Bible that God frequently rejected the prayers of His ancient people Israel because of their insincerity. All formalists should remember the stern warning of Jesus and the prophets: "This people honoreth me with their lips; But their heart is far from me" (Matt. 15:8, ASV). When you pray you must learn to pray earnestly and sincerely. Some people hesitate to pray because they think that their grammar is not good enough or that their vocabulary is too limited. We should put our prayers in the best language we know, especially our audible prayers, but God does not listen for grammar and diction. God is listening for words that come from the heart. Send your prayers to the throne from a sincere heart and you will please God.

A second mark of the prayer that God hears is humility and reverence. When we pray we must always remember who we are. We must remember that we are creatures before the Creator. We must remember that we are redeemed sinners whose only claim to be heard is the mercy and grace of God. We need to remember that we speak to the Creator and Ruler of this vast universe. We do well to hold before us the example of Abraham who came to God saying, "Behold now, I have taken upon me to speak unto the Lord, who am but dust and ashes" (Gen. 18:27).

The third mark of the prayer God hears is faith. How often Jesus said to those who came to Him for help during His earthly ministry, "Be it done unto you according to your faith." Perhaps you are asking, "But how can I get this confidence and assurance? When I pray I have no feeling at all that God will hear and answer me. It is faith and confidence that I need but where do I get it?" You get it in Jesus. It is your sinful heart that keeps you from trusting God. It is sin that fills our minds with doubts even as we phrase our petitions. Because of our sinfulness we need a Mediator, and if we come to God through the Mediator, through Jesus Christ, the one Mediator appointed by God as our way to Him, we will have boldness and confidence in Him. There is no other name than the name of Jesus that will give us access to God. "Having therefore, brethren, boldness to enter into the holy place by the blood of Jesus, by the way which he dedicated for us, a new and living way . . . let us draw near with a true heart in fulness of faith" (Heb. 10:19, 20, 22, ASV). Pray to God in the name of Jesus and He will hear you. When your heart fails you for fear, and when doubts arise, look to Jesus, the Mediator, and He will give you courage to pray on, to pray through to victory.

# Chapter II

# TO WHOM SHOULD WE PRAY?

*"Our Father who art in heaven . . ."*
(Matthew 6:9)

In this second meditation on the Lord's Prayer we will observe how Jesus answers the question: To whom should we pray? In the introduction to the prayer Jesus taught His disciples, He gave a clear answer to that question when He said, "After this manner therefore pray ye: Our Father who art in heaven."/This shows that our prayers must be addressed to the one true God, the Father of our Lord Jesus Christ. He is revealed to us in Scripture, and in Jesus Christ, as the Creator of heaven and earth, the Father and Creator of all mankind, the one Being who rules heaven and earth from His throne of power and glory, and who is our heavenly Father. We learn therefore that our prayers must be addressed to God, our Father, who is in heaven.

This takes us to a study of the opening sentence of the Lord's Prayer: "Our Father who art in heaven." Let us begin our study of this part of the Lord's Prayer by/considering the instruction that there is in the words "our Father." What do we mean when we address God as Father, and by what right do we so address God?

Because there has been some very loose thinking in our day about the Fatherhood of God we must begin by observing one of the/basic distinctions in the Bible. This is the distinction between the Fatherhood of creation and the Fatherhood of redemption. The Bible teaches that God is the Father of all men by

17

creation. He is the Author of our being. All men are created in the image of God. When Paul preached to the pagan Greeks at Athens, the first part of his message was based on the fact of creation. "The God that made the world and all things therein, he, being Lord of heaven and earth, dwelleth not in temples made with hands; neither is he served by men's hands, as though he needed anything, seeing he himself giveth to all life, and breath, and all things; and he made of one every nation of men to dwell on all the face of the earth, having determined their appointed seasons, and the bounds of their habitation; that they should seek God, if haply they might feel after him and find him, though he is not far from each one of us; for in him we live, and move, and have our being" (Acts 17:24-28, ASV).

The teaching of the Bible about providence and preservation is based on the Fatherhood of creation. Jesus taught that God cares for and provides for the needs of all men. He said that God makes the sun to rise on the evil and the good, and that He sends the rain on the just and the unjust (Matt. 5:45). The seasons of the year, the sunshine and the rain, the fruit of the tree and the field, the life of the sea are all under the government of God for the welfare of man. God provides for and sustains all His creatures even though they have forfeited all right to His goodness and care. You may recall that Jesus said that God is kind to the unthankful and evil. When we speak of God as our Father, therefore, we are reminded that we are all His children by creation.

But God is a saving Father only to those who are redeemed. Because man has forfeited the privilege of sonship he must be restored by grace. The Bible reveals a new sonship, a new relationship between the sinner and the Creator. This is the sonship which is created in Jesus Christ. "But as many as received him, to them gave he the right to become children of God, even to them that believe on his name" (John 1:12, ASV).

We become true redeemed children of God only by adoption and regeneration. It was necessary for God to adopt us by grace, because we became aliens from the family of God through sin.

It is only through redemption that we acquire the rights of the children of God and become the heirs of God. Through sin man not only forfeited his rights and his position as a child of God, but his nature also became corrupt. As a result of man's fall in sin he is no longer a true and obedient child of God but is inclined by nature to hate God and his neighbor. This is why we must all be born again. Our corrupt nature must be renewed so that we do love God and obey Him. We see therefore that when God becomes our Father through redemption, He does two things: by adoption He restores us to the position of sonship, and by regeneration He gives us a new nature which enables us to live in obedience to God and causes us to love God and our neighbor.

Let us now consider what bearing this knowledge of the Fatherhood of God has on our prayers. For one thing, this teaches us that we have access to God in prayer. Because we have a Mediator, Jesus Christ, it is possible for us to speak to God as our Father. Let me remind you of the wonder of it. Consider the greatness of God: His majesty, His holiness, His power. God is the Creator and the Ruler of the universe. You know how hard it is to see a great man in industry, or in government. It is almost impossible to get past all the secretaries in order to see the man in his own private office. Have you ever thought of the wonder of being able to approach God, the Creator and the Ruler of all the nations of the world? Furthermore, we have forfeited all our rights of access to God because of sin. We have rebelled against God and we have given up the right to call Him our Father. The glory and wonder of the Gospel is that we who are sinners by nature can call God our Father. Through the atoning death of Jesus Christ on the cross we are restored to sonship. Every time we pray and say "our Father" we are reminded that the Creator of heaven and earth is ready to hear us and to answer us. This is the wonder of God's grace. He hears the cry of all His children who call upon Him through the Mediator Jesus Christ.

The words "our Father" also give us trust and confidence when we come to Him in prayer. Jesus teaches us to say "our Father" so that at the very beginning of our prayer we may be reminded of the goodness of God and His readiness to hear us. We should begin our prayers with the confidence of children who come to their father. All doubts about God's goodness are driven away when we say "our Father." To call God Father reminds us that if we who are evil know how to give good gifts unto our children, how much more will our heavenly Father give good things to those who ask Him (Matt. 7:11).

We are encouraged to pray because we know that God hears and answers our prayers, but this must not be construed to mean that He will give us everything we ask for. The goodness of God in hearing and answering our petitions is the goodness of an all-wise Father, not the superficial goodness of a weak or doting earthly father. Even on earth a good father often denies the request of his children, and when he denies the request he does it for the welfare of the child. Every father knows that there are times when he must say "No" to the request of a child for the child's own good. When God our Father in heaven denies a request it is for our ultimate good.

The Fatherhood of God expressed in the Lord's Prayer is primarily the Fatherhood of redemption. Only God's redeemed children can claim His attention. This is not to say that God never hears the prayer of an unregenerate sinner. The 107th Psalm and other passages of Scripture make abundantly clear that sinful men sometimes cry to God and in His goodness He hears them. But only God's redeemed children have a right to be heard. Only those who are God's children by grace and the new birth can rest upon the promises of the Bible.

In this sense the Lord's Prayer is the believer's prayer. It is a prayer for Christians. Does this exclude anyone? Perhaps you are not a Christian. Have I excluded you by saying that the Lord's Prayer is only for believers? When we say that the Lord's Prayer is a prayer for Christians, we only point you to the same gate by which we came in. We who are Christians are only sinners saved by grace. Through repentance and faith you too can come to Jesus and become a child of God. If there were a free public dinner to which the whole town was invited and you came and found a barricade between you and the people who were within the hall eating, would you say that you were excluded? Would you lean over the barricade and say to one of your friends at the table that you were left out? Your friend sitting at the dinner would merely point to the entrance and say, "Come in through the gate, there is still room." To say that the Lord's Prayer is the believer's prayer is not exclusive or narrow. It merely points all men to the door, Jesus Christ. Come to Jesus now, enter through Him and you too can call God your Father.

Having considered the meaning of the Fatherhood of God, let us now look at the whole phrase and consider the instruction in the words "our Father." You notice that Jesus did not teach us to pray "my Father," although there are times when we can so personally address God. In the prayer which He taught the disciples we are to say "our Father." In this we acknowledge, first of all, the universality of God's power and goodness. He is the God of the whole earth, of every people, tribe and nation. When we pray "our Father" we are to put from our minds any narrow, national, racial, family or personal exclusiveness. Our Father is the God of the whole earth.

The plural pronoun "our" also reminds us that we are not the only children of God. This part of the prayer teaches us to remember our brethren. When we pray for bread we must pray for our brother's bread. This address made to God when I pray the Lord's Prayer reminds me as a Christian that it is not only my fears, not only my sins, not only my needs, but my brother's needs, my brother's sins, and my brother's sorrows that I am to bring before the throne of grace. We are not to weep alone but we are to share each other's sorrows and joys whenever we come to the throne of grace in prayer. This address also reminds us of our spiritual union. Whatever may be the will of God about the external union of the churches, here is a true union we dare not forget. Christians are taught to say "our Father." All those who are in Jesus Christ are brethren. Here is the communion of saints. "We are not divided, all one body we."

This prayer should also remind us that the oneness and the love which we have in Christ Jesus, which we express in the very invocation of our prayers, must be reflected in our daily action. If we are one in Christ we must show our unity in love and kindness to one another.

Let us now consider the meaning of the words "in heaven." Jesus taught us to say, "Our Father who art in heaven." What does the Bible mean by heaven and what does it mean to say that God is in heaven? Someone may say, Doesn't the Bible teach that God is everywhere? and quote Psalm 139 which says, "Whither shall I go from thy spirit? or whither shall I flee from thy presence? If I ascend up into heaven, thou art there: if I make my bed in hell, behold, thou art there. If I take the wings of the morning, and dwell in the uttermost parts of the sea; Even there shall thy hand lead me, and thy right hand shall hold me" (7-10). It is true that God is everywhere but the Bible teaches that there is a place where the majesty and the glory of God is more clearly revealed than in any other. This is called heaven. Heaven is the throne of God and His dwelling place. He is there praised and served by the blessed angels and all the saints and redeemed who stand around His throne.

Daniel describes a vision God gave him of the eternal order: "I beheld till thrones were placed, and one that was ancient of days did sit: his raiment was white as snow, and the hair of his head like pure wool; his throne was fiery flames, and the wheels thereof burning fire. A fiery stream issued and came forth from before him: thousands of thousands ministered unto him, and ten thousand times ten thousand stood before him: the judgment was set, and the books were opened" (7:9, 10, ASV).

Heaven is the place where God sits on His throne. The word *heaven* occurs twice in the Lord's Prayer — once, in the invocation where we say, "Our Father who art in heaven," and again in the third petition, where we say, "Thy will be done in earth, as it is in heaven." This makes it plain that if earth is a place, then heaven is a place also.

This part of the Lord's Prayer in which we address God as our Father who is in heaven reminds us when we pray of the majesty and the power of God. The word *heaven* in this prayer suggests the dominion and power of God. Heaven is higher than the whole world, therefore the word *heaven* in the Lord's Prayer is intended to remind us of God's almightiness.

The word *heaven* is also intended to increase our reverence toward God. God is our Father, but He is our Father in heaven. By the word *heaven* we are reminded of His holiness and His majesty. The old writers speak of a proper mixture of fear and humility. The words "our Father in heaven" give us the proper balance between fear and hope in our prayer, for the word *Father* reminds us of God's goodness and grace, and the word *heaven* reminds us of His power and authority. The words "our Father in heaven" teach us that in prayer we come to One who is perfectly good and who has all power to meet every need. Therefore when you pray lift your mind from earth to heaven. Remember that you speak to God; He is your Father, you can trust Him; He is in heaven. He has all power to supply every need.

# Chapter III

# REVERENCE IN PRAYER

*"Hallowed be thy name."*
(Matthew 6:9)

So far in this series of meditations on prayer we have studied the teaching of Jesus on the necessity and nature of prayer. Now we begin a study of another of the basic problems of prayer: What are the proper things to pray for? Jesus answered that question when He said, "After this manner therefore pray ye," giving us what we now call the Lord's Prayer. In the six petitions of this prayer He gave a complete summary of the things we should pray for. A careful study of these petitions will show how comprehensive they are. We must make a full study of each petition before we really understand what are the right and proper things to pray for.

Calvin says, "Written in this formula which has been handed down from the best Master is everything which we must ask from God and in general can ask. And this prayer is in every way so perfect that whatever foreign and alien element is added to it but cannot be traced back to it, is impious and is unworthy to be heard by God." Calvin with his characteristic insight into the Word of God saw in the model prayer of Jesus not only what we should include in our prayers but also what must be excluded from them as unworthy subjects for prayer. This is also what Luther meant when he said, "A Christian has prayed abundantly who has rightly prayed the Lord's Prayer."

As we begin our study of the main part of the Lord's Prayer, let us consider, first, the order of the petitions. The six petitions of the Lord's Prayer are divided into two parts. In the first three we ask for the honor and glory of God, and in the last three we ask for the needs of man. In the first three petitions, "Hallowed be thy name," "thy kingdom come," "thy will be done," we pray for the honor of God, for the coming of His kingdom, and ask that His will may be done on earth as it is in heaven. It is not until we come to the fourth petition, "Give us this day our daily bread," that we begin to pray for our own needs.

We observe from the order of the petitions in the Lord's Prayer that God and His kingdom are first, and man and his needs second. This is one of the first lessons we need to learn in our time about religion. We need to know that our need for God and our duty towards God comes first. Some time ago an article appeared in one of the large daily newspapers of Chicago in which forty-three young men, who signed themselves as "future ministers," criticized the church and said that it was missing the boat because it did not gear its program to the working man. A few days later there appeared a letter in the readers' column of that same newspaper, objecting that these forty-three young men did not understand even the fundamentals of religion. This correspondent wrote that when she went to church she wanted her soul lifted up to God. The real trouble today with so many churches is that their whole program centers in man. The so-called social gospel of the first half of the twentieth century was based on a view of religion which would make the first and only petition in our prayers, Give us this day our daily bread. It is becoming apparent that this social gospel was the half-way house to a purely secular society.

The increasing secularization of our way of life is reflected in an article on Sunday selling which appeared in *Time* magazine recently. The article gave a number of incidents to show that Sunday is rapidly becoming the biggest day for selling in the retail business. In many of the metropolitan areas more than 50% of the cars are sold on Sunday. In spite of vigorous objections

from church and business groups, the Lord's day, as a day of rest
and worship, is rapidly disappearing from the American scene.
The complete secularization of our modern way of life is summed
up in the comment of a Cleveland housewife on Sunday shopping,
"Getting up late Sunday and shopping with the kids after a slow
breakfast is fun. It's like going to the fair." Someone ought to
tell this poor little housewife that with the complete exclusion
of God from life it will be like going to Vanity Fair. The only
cure for this secular view of life is found in a return to the living
God with the recognition of His authority and His rule. We find
that in the Lord's Prayer. We learn from this prayer that the chief
end of man is to honor and glorify God and enjoy Him forever.
The order of the petitions in the Lord's Prayer teaches the same
lesson as the injunction, "Seek ye first the kingdom of God and
his righteousness and all these things shall be added unto you."
The order of the Bible in putting God first is the right order
and needs to be restored in our time. There is no other way to
peace and righteousness and contentment. God who is the creator
and ruler of the world is the source of all life and of all our
blessings. The organization of man's life apart from God results
in disorder, confusion and strife. This is evident in our time.
Deny God and His authority, and the result is disorder and chaos.

If we follow the order Jesus taught us in this prayer, putting
God and His kingdom first, it will solve many of the so-called
problems of prayer. The order of the petitions teaches us that
we must love God for Himself and not first of all for His gifts.
We are to love Him because He is our Father and not only and
primarily because He can help us, or do something for us, or
satisfy our wants and desires. Is there any way a child can hurt
his father more than by giving the impression that he loves his
father and is obedient to him only because of what his father
can give him? Does a child really love his father if his only interest in him is for the food, clothes, and money he can give him?
Let us learn to love and adore God for Himself, because He is

our Father in heaven. In that spirit we are to pray, "Our Father who art in heaven, Hallowed be thy name."

We are not to think that seeking the honor and the glory of God and His kingdom is something apart from ourselves. We are the children of God. Because we are His children it is for our ultimate good that His name should be hallowed and that the will of God be done on earth as it is in heaven. Every petition of the Lord's Prayer is for our good. A seventeenth century writer points this out in a very good summary of the Lord's Prayer. After showing that all our wants are included in these petitions he says, "We cannot ask more than all. If 'God's name be sanctified' we are holy. If 'his kingdom come' we reign as kings. If 'his will be done' we are saved; for his will is our salvation. If 'he gives us our daily bread' our souls do live to praise him. If 'he forgive us our sins' no evil past — if 'he lead us not into temptation, but deliver us from evil' no evil to come — can hurt us" (Farindon).

The order of the petitions of the Lord's Prayer which requires us to put God and His kingdom first, teaches us also that our spiritual needs come before our physical needs. Holiness and obedience come before our daily bread. William Thackeray's *Vanity Fair* is generally regarded as one of the great novels of the English language. This novel, as the title indicates, exposes the vanity and the emptiness of life when it is lived without regard for God or man's immortal soul. Speaking of those who sneer at the practice of devotions, Thackeray says that the laughter comes from those "who have no reverence except for prosperity and no eye for anything beyond success." The study of the Lord's Prayer gives us an opportunity to put some searching questions to ourselves as to what we value and what we reverence.

Let us now consider what we ask for when we pray, "Hallowed be thy name." It should be observed that this is not a doxology or an adoration, though by inference we may find praise in it. This is first of all a petition. Just as we ask for the coming of the kingdom, and ask that God's will may be done, so we are taught to ask that the name of God be hallowed. To hallow means to honor, glorify and reverence the name of God. This does not mean that God's name is not holy already, or that it can be made holy by our prayer. The meaning of the petition is well stated by Augustine who observed:/"This is prayed for, not as if God's name were not holy already, but that it may be held holy by men."

When we pray, "Hallowed be thy name" we ask that all men may hallow, or honor, the name of God. This is therefore a prayer that the name of God may be known./The first petition of the Lord's Prayer is a <u>missionary prayer</u>. It is a prayer for the increase of the knowledge of the true God.'It is a prayer for God's blessing upon the preaching of His Word by which the knowledge of God is spread abroad throughout the whole wide earth./It is grounded in the great promises of the Old Testament. The 72nd Psalm is a prophecy that the name of God will be known and honored everywhere. This Psalm describes the reign of the righteous King, and ends with the prediction, <u>"His name shall endure for ever; his name shall be continued as long as the sun; and men shall be blessed in him; all nations shall call him blessed.</u>" Following this prophecy is one of the doxologies of the Psalter. /'Blessed be the Lord God, the God of Israel, who only doeth wondrous things. And blessed be his glorious name for ever; <u>and let the whole earth be filled with his glory</u>; Amen, and Amen" (Psalm 72:18, 19). If in ancient Israel, when God was known in only one nation and His Word preached in only one language, there was such faith in the universal spread of the knowledge of God, with how much more confidence and assurance should we preach the Gospel and pray that the God and Father of our Lord Jesus Christ may be known and honored by all men!

"Hallowed be thy name" is also a <u>personal prayer</u>. It is an expression of desire. It is a prayer for pure motives and for a pure heart. Will you reflect for a moment on your own practice of prayer? How many of your personal prayers are concerned with the glory of God, and how often have you prayed to God that His name be reverenced and made holy in your own life and in your own heart? This is a very practical petition for it will cure personal jealousy. The more we desire God's glory and honor the less we will be concerned with our own.

Let us now consider some of the ways that God's name may be hallowed. If we earnestly pray for the honor of the name of God we should also work for the glory and honor of God's name. How is God's name hallowed?

First of all by public worship. When we gather together in God's house for public worship and praise we honor God's name. Speaking to Israel through the prophet Micah, God asks, "If I am a Father, where is my honor?" One of the first reasons for public worship is for the honor and the glory of God. We too often look at worship from a selfish point of view. Too many ask, "What do I get out of it?" Have you ever thought of going to church for the glory of God? To sing praises to His name and to bring your personal offering for the work of God? God is honored in public worship. The enemies of God and the Gospel do all they can in a totalitarian state to stamp out public worship. They know that the very announcement of such a service, and an assembly in the name of Christ, increases the knowledge and the honor of God among men.

Secondly, we hallow the name of God by the observance of the Lord's day. See how closely the name of God and the Lord's day are related. The third commandment is: "Thou shalt not take the name of the Lord thy God in vain"; the fourth commandment is: "Remember the Sabbath Day to keep it holy." God's name and God's day are directly related in Scripture, and when we profane the Lord's day we profane the Lord's name. It is inconsistent to pray that God's name may be hallowed, and then deliberately to desecrate the Lord's day by using it for personal pleasure or profit.

We should hallow the name of God in our daily speech. The opposite of sanctifying or hallowing the name of God is profaning it. How can we pray, "Hallowed be thy name" and take His name in vain in our daily talk? Profanity makes a mockery of the Lord's Prayer. To honor God in our speech does not mean merely that we avoid profanity; it means that we should use every opportunity in our daily conversation to/describe the things that happen to us from a Christian point of view. We do well to consider our hesitation to speak of the things of God and ask if we are ashamed of the Gospel of Jesus Christ. If you have a narrow escape do you say, "I was lucky"? or do you say, "God spared my life"? As we continue to pray, "Hallowed be thy name," let us also study to make our speech a natural and sincere expression of our desire to promote the glory of God.

4) We must hallow the name of God in our daily life. The name of God is hallowed by the holiness of His people. When Jesus set forth the principles by which His disciples were to live He summed it all up by saying, "Even so let your light shine before men that they may see your good works and glorify your Father who is in heaven" (Matt. 5:16, ASV).

John Keble wrote two weighty lines about prayer:

> *And teach us this and every day*
> *To live more nearly as we pray.*

If we honor God in public worship, if we keep His day holy, if we honor the name of God in our speech, if we live an obedient and holy life, then we can pray from the heart, "Our Father which art in heaven, Hallowed be thy name."

# Chapter IV

# PRAYER FOR THE COMING OF THE KINGDOM

*"Thy kingdom come."*
(Matthew 6:10)

The prayer for the coming of God's kingdom is the shortest petition in the Lord's Prayer but one of the most profound. We see the importance and the magnitude of this petition when we recall that the kingdom of God was the central theme of the preaching and teaching of Jesus.

Jesus began His ministry by proclaiming: "The time is fulfilled and the kingdom of God is at hand: repent ye, and believe the gospel" (Mark 1:15). In the Sermon on the Mount He laid down the laws of the kingdom. He spoke of the kingdom His last night on earth when He was with His disciples in the upper room. When He instituted the Lord's Supper He said, "Take this and divide it among yourselves: for I say unto you I will not drink of the fruit of the vine, until the kingdom of God shall come" (Luke 22:17, 18). When Jesus was nailed to the cross they put this inscription over His head, "This is the King of the Jews," and from that cross He promised a dying thief immediate entrance into the kingdom. After He arose from the dead He showed Himself alive to His disciples by many infallible proofs, and for forty days spoke of the things concerning the kingdom of God (Acts 1:3). From the opening message of Jesus' ministry through the glorious forty days on earth after His resurrection, the kingdom of God was central in His teaching.

This brief survey of the ministry of Jesus shows us that in order to understand the meaning of these words of the Lord's Prayer, "Thy kingdom come," we should know, first, What is the nature of the kingdom of God? and second, What is meant by praying for the kingdom of God to come?

Although we cannot fully expound the nature of the kingdom of God in this brief meditation, it will be very helpful for our knowledge of the Lord's Prayer and the petition, "Thy kingdom come," if we understand a few of the most important facts about the kingdom of God.

The first is that the kingdom of God is a spiritual kingdom. Jesus was brought to trial before the Roman judge of His province because He had said that He was a king and because He spoke of establishing a kingdom. When Pilate questioned Him about this charge, Jesus declared that He was a king, and at the same time defined the nature of the kingdom. Jesus said, "My kingdom is not of this world" (John 18:36). In that one sentence Jesus summed up the first fact about the kingdom of God. It is a spiritual kingdom. When Jesus said, "My kingdom is not of this world," He meant that it is not a temporal kingdom supported by military power and maintained by taxes. He also made it clear that the kingdom of God is not concerned with the pleasures and the selfish interests of this world. "The kingdom of God is not meat and drink; but righteousness, and peace, and joy in the Holy Ghost" (Romans 14:17).

Because the kingdom of God is not of this world, because it is a spiritual kingdom, it may be inferred that it is not advanced by the methods of the world. It is a spiritual kingdom advanced primarily by spiritual means. There is a tendency today to organize the church and to promote the cause of Christ by means which have been successful in big business. There must be order and intelligence in carrying on the work of the Lord, but we must also remember that a spiritual kingdom is advanced by spiritual means. The kingdom of God is the rule of God over the will and heart and conscience of man, and that kind of kingdom can be advanced only by spiritual means. There is very little information in the New Testament about the organization and government of the church; but there is very much in the New Testament to show us how the kingdom of God was advanced. The Gospel writers tell us that Jesus came preaching and that the apostles went everywhere preaching the Gospel. They proclaimed to all who would hear that salvation had come to the world through the death and resurrection of Jesus Christ. The Gospel writers also tell us that Jesus was a man of prayer and that He taught His disciples to pray. Jesus prayed before He healed the sick, before He appointed the Twelve, and before He raised the dead. He arose early in the morning to pray, and He sometimes prayed all night. His example ought to remind us today that the kingdom of God is advanced by prayer. Preaching and praying are spiritual exercises and are the primary means by which the kingdom of God is advanced.

The second fact that stands out in the Gospels is that the kingdom of God is both present and future. There are many passages in the Gospels which indicate that the kingdom had come in Jesus' day. Jesus Himself said, "The kingdom of God is at hand." He said that some who heard Him speak would not taste of death until they should see the kingdom of God (Luke 9:27). He said, "But if I by the finger of God cast out demons, then is the kingdom of God come upon you" (Luke 11:20, ASV). It is clear from this and many other passages in the Gospels that the kingdom of God in all its saving power was present in His person and in His teaching. It had already come to Israel in the ministry of Jesus. It is certainly plain enough in the New Testament that Jesus and the apostles preached the kingdom of God as a reality present in their time.

On the other hand, there are many passages in the Gospels which speak of the kingdom of God as still to come. "For I say unto you, I shall not drink from henceforth of the fruit of the vine, until the kingdom of God shall come" (Luke 22:18, ASV). "And as they heard these things, he added and spake a parable, because he was nigh to Jerusalem, and because they supposed that the kingdom of God was immediately to appear" (Luke 19:11, ASV). These passages, and many others, make it clear that the kingdom of God will come in fullness and power with the coming of the King in power and glory. It is clear therefore that the kingdom of God is both present and future. In one sense it is here now: in another it is still to come.

(3)  In Christian theology these two aspects of the kingdom of God have been distinguished by the terms "kingdom of grace" and "kingdom of glory." This is not to say that there are two kingdoms. There is only one kingdom of God, but in the sense that the kingdom of God and His saving power have come to man in Jesus Christ, the kingdom of God is the kingdom of grace and it is here now. Because there are many promises of God in the Old Testament, as well as in the New, which are not yet fulfilled, because we have not yet seen the fullness of power and glory God has promised to His people, we speak of glory still to come.

The kingdom of God therefore viewed as the kingdom of grace is the present salvation that God brings in Jesus Christ. The kingdom of God comes for a particular person when his heart is renewed and yielded to God and fully obedient to Him. This is the meaning of the teaching of the Bible that you must be born again to enter the kingdom of God. Where God dwells in man's heart by faith and Christ reigns by love, the kingdom of God has come. This reign of God in the heart of man is called a kingdom because there are many who have been born again. The word *kingdom* suggests society, order, allegiance to a throne, and obedience to authority. All these are found in the redeemed children of God who do His will on earth.

(4)  Because the kingdom of God has to do with salvation it may be asked, What is the relation of the kingdom of God to the Christian Church? A study of the New Testament will show that there is the closest possible relation between the two. We will understand that relation a little better if we remember a very important distinction in the concept of the church which was

made by the Reformers. They distinguished between the form and the essence of the church and spoke of a church visible and of a church invisible. By the church visible they meant the institution of the church. The visible church is the church we can see, that is, the organization and the membership of the church. By the church invisible they meant the redeemed children of God, the elect, those who are truly saved. The church invisible, in the sense of the regenerate, is identical with the kingdom of God considered as the kingdom of grace. The visible church, that is, the church that is organized to carry on the work of God, is best thought of as the primary agency of the kingdom.

Let us consider next what is meant by the coming of the kingdom of God and what we ask for when we pray, "Thy kingdom come." We must remember that this is a petition, and that we ask that God may bring in the kingdom. From the survey we have just made on the meaning of the kingdom, we may observe that to pray "Thy kingdom come" is to pray, first of all, for conversions. The kingdom of God comes to a particular person when he repents and believes the Gospel, when he receives the Lord Jesus Christ by faith. This act makes him a new person. He recognizes the supremacy of God in his life. He is obedient to God and yields his will to the will of God. To pray for the kingdom of God to come therefore is to pray for the kingdom of God to come into the hearts of men. It is to pray that many may hear the Gospel of Jesus Christ and be converted, to become renewed children of God. The kingdom of God has not come for you and never will until you receive Christ Jesus as your Saviour. If you do not receive Christ by faith you are excluded from the kingdom of God. On the other hand, this prayer can be fulfilled in your life in this moment if you will bow down and ask God to forgive your sins. If you will humble yourself before Him, if you will put your trust in Jesus Christ and His death on the cross alone for your salvation, you too will become a child of God and the kingdom of God will come for you. Remember the word of Jesus to Nicodemus, "Verily, verily, I say unto thee, Except a man be born again, he cannot see the kingdom of God" (John 3:3). You must be born again before the kingdom of God comes to you.

To pray for the coming of the kingdom is not only to pray for conversions; this is also a prayer for believers. It is a prayer for Christians. For those who already know Christ it is a prayer that they may grow in grace and obedience. Our hearts are renewed if we are Christians but they are not yet made perfect. We must confess that often there is rebellion in our heart. We must confess to lust, to self will, to evil thoughts and evil desires. Every Christian who is honest with himself must confess that he still has a long way to go before he lives a life that is in perfect obedience to the will of God. To that extent to pray, "Thy kingdom come," is a prayer for a heart that is more fully yielded to the will of God and a life more completely devoted to the service of God and to the glory of God. It is to pray for a fuller obedience to the will of God and to His commandments.

> O for a heart to praise my God!
> A heart from sin set free;
> A heart that always feels Thy blood,
> So freely shed for me.
> A heart in every thought renewed,
> And full of love divine,
> Perfect, and right, and pure, and good,
> A copy, Lord, of Thine.

"Thy kingdom come" means bringing every thought into captivity to the obedience of Christ. "Casting down imaginations, and every high thing that is exalted against the knowledge of God, and bringing every thought into captivity to the obedience of Christ" (II Cor. 10:5, ASV).

To pray, "Thy kingdom come" means further that we pray for the preaching of the Gospel and for the increase of the knowledge of God and of the Gospel of Jesus Christ. It is to pray that the nations of the world may be brought to Jesus Christ. Let us learn to look to the spreading of the Gospel as an extension of

God's kingdom. The kingdom of God is the only hope for the world. The only way to peace is that all men shall recognize the righteous and gracious rule of God. Therefore pray fervently for the coming of the kingdom of God.

The sincerity and fervency of our desire for the kingdom of God to come will be measured also by our work and our giving for the kingdom. A few years ago when speaking at a Bible conference the chairman of one of the meetings called on an elder he knew to close with prayer. The elder offered an earnest prayer for the work of the Gospel and the extension of the kingdom, and prayed fervently for God's blessing on Temple Time. About an hour after the meeting was dismissed the chairman came to me and said, "Here is $50.00 for the radio broadcast." I asked, "Where did you get that?" He said, "From the man who prayed this morning. He stopped me after the meeting and said, 'Here is a gift for Temple Time. I never pray for a cause without giving to it.'"

Do you really long for God's kingdom to come? Do you believe it is the only hope of the world? Then pray, and to your prayers add your gifts and your labors. Serve God actively in your church and in your community. The sincerity and effectiveness of our prayers for the coming of God's kingdom on earth is measured also by our work for the kingdom. What are you doing in your community for the cause of righteousness? Our society is far from Christian. There are serious injustices in our social order. We still fall far short of the standards of righteousness of the kingdom of God. We must not only pray, "Thy kingdom come," but in our daily life we must work for that kingdom by working for righteousness in our community.

Recently I heard the story of two little girls who were on their way to school on a rainy day. They were a little late, so one girl suggested that they sit down and pray that they might make it. But the second little girl said, "No, we had better run and pray too." The religion of Jesus Christ teaches us that if we are ever to have a Christian social order, we must pray, "Thy kingdom come," but at the same time we must work for the coming of His kingdom. Consider the injunction Jesus laid on us in the Sermon on the Mount around the central theme, "Ye are the salt of the earth and the light of the world."

 Finally, to pray, "Thy kingdom come" is to pray for the personal return of the Lord Jesus Christ. The kingdom will come in fullness and in glory when the King comes back. The kingdom of God must come from above, and it will come completely and perfectly only with the coming of our Lord and Saviour Jesus Christ. Then the kingdoms of this world will become the kingdom of our Lord and of His Christ; and He shall reign for ever and ever (Rev. 11:15). Can you pray from the heart, "Thy kingdom come"? Do you long for the Lord to come? Or, are you afraid lest His coming should interrupt your business, or interfere with your plans for your family, or your career? After this when you pray, "Thy kingdom come," think of it as a prayer for the coming of the Lord Jesus Christ. Pray from the heart as the early Christians did, "Even so, come, Lord Jesus, come." Learn with them to cry, "Maranatha, O Lord, come."

# CHAPTER V

# PRAYER AND THE WILL OF GOD

*"Thy will be done in earth, as it is in heaven."*
(MATTHEW 6:10)

We come to the heart of the matter between God and ourselves in this petition of the Lord's Prayer. The end or purpose of life is to be found in the will of God. A few years ago in a church I was serving we had a farewell missionary service for a young man and his wife who were going to the foreign field for the first time. They were going to a very primitive tribe in the heart of Africa. We have other missionaries working in this tribe in Africa and so our congregation knew something about what life in the South Sudan would be like for this young couple. As the missionary and his attractive young wife with their three-year-old daughter mingled through the congregation before the meeting began, many of the people in the church spoke of the great sacrifice this young couple was making in leaving their home and their friends to go into the heart of Africa to live and preach the Gospel of Jesus Christ. When it was time for the missionary to speak a word of farewell, he began by commenting on the fact that so many people had spoken of the sacrifice that they were making in going to Africa. He said that he wanted to hear no more about what they were giving up and leaving behind; he said they were going to Africa because they believed that to be the will of God for their lives, and then he added, "The sweetest thing in the world is to be in the will of God."

41

I recalled this incident some time later when I was reading a news account of the death of the/managing editor of one of the most brazen tabloid newspapers of an era of gaudy and sensational journalism. In his memoirs, the editor left an epitaph in which he said:|"I was part of that strange race of people, aptly described as spending their lives doing things they detest, to make money they don't want, to buy things they don't need, to impress people they dislike." The difference between these two men lies in their knowledge of and their concern to be in the will of God. We learn what our relation to the will of God ought to be from the prayer Jesus taught us when He said, "After this manner therefore pray ye: Our Father who art in heaven . . . Thy will be done, as in heaven so on earth."

As we study this part of the Lord's Prayer, we should observe that it contains two parts: there is first a petition — "Thy will be done" — and second a pattern — "as in heaven, so on earth." As we look at the petition, first, it may be asked,|"How can we know what the will of God is?" In answer to that question, I would like to call your attention to a distinction which is usually made in Christian theology between God's/secret (or His absolute) will and His revealed will. This is a valid distinction and we must be reminded of it when we pray, "Thy will be done." In the book of Deuteronomy, in the Old Testament, we read that the secret things belong unto the Lord our God but the things that are revealed belong to us and to our children./The will of God that we ask to be done in the Lord's Prayer is His revealed will. This is the will that God has revealed for man in His commandments, in His Word, and finally and fully in the Gospel, and in His Son, Jesus Christ.

We should also note that the will of God for which we pray is the will of the living God, who is holy and good. It is not the will of an unknown power we are to obey, it is not an arbitrary tyrannous will, it is the will of our Father in heaven who loves us and who wills our good. Our God and Father does not rule by whim or caprice. He has revealed Himself in His Word as a

God of love and righteousness. We must observe, therefore, that the will that we pray may be done on earth as it is in heaven is the will of a holy, righteous God whose name is Love.

In order to understand this petition better, we should also know how the will of God must be done. What is meant by doing God's will? We learn from the Bible that this means at least three things. First of all, to do the will of God means to keep His commandments. It means to live in obedience to His Word. In the Bible God tells us what He wants us to do and how He wants us to live. The moral message of the Word of God can be summed up in two words: "do right." This shows us how practical and down-to-earth this subject really is. The will of God is against dishonesty, impurity, adultery, gossip, lying and hatred. Here is a sample passage from the New Testament. "For this ye know, that no whoremonger, nor unclean person, nor covetous man, who is an idolater, hath any inheritance in the kingdom of Christ and of God. Let no man deceive you with vain words: for because of these things cometh the wrath of God upon the children of disobedience" (Eph. 5:5, 6).

But God reveals Himself and His will to us not only in His Word and in His commandments, but in His own Son. God sent His Son, Jesus Christ, into this world that men might know God and His will. When Jesus Christ was on this earth, God the Father Himself testified that Christ was His Son and declared from heaven, "This is my beloved Son, hear ye him." The will of God, therefore, for all mankind is that they should come to Him through Jesus Christ and be saved. No man can be said to live within the will of God until he knows Jesus Christ as his Lord and Saviour. If you pray "Thy will be done" then remember that the will of God for your life is that you should repent and believe in Jesus Christ and walk in His way. The will of God, therefore, for each one of us begins in the confession of our sins and in turning to Him in repentance and faith. The Bible says, "But without faith it is impossible to please him: for he that cometh to God must believe that he is, and that he is a rewarder of them that diligently seek him" (Heb. 11:6). This faith which leads us to God and salvation must be expressed in obedience. Jesus said, "Not every one that saith unto me, Lord, Lord, shall enter into the kingdom of heaven; but he that doeth the will of my Father who is in heaven" (Matt. 7:21). At another time Jesus recognized kinship only with those who obey God. "For whosoever shall do the will of my Father who is in heaven, he is my brother, and sister, and mother" (Matt. 12:50, ASV).

The third way in which we do the will of God is by our submission to His will in the providential circumstances of our lives. To do God's will means to accept His will for your life. The teaching of the Bible about the kingdom of God and the will of God shows us that nothing happens by chance. God is the sovereign ruler of all. Because nothing happens by chance but everything happens by the will of our God and Father, we must learn to trust Him in whatever He sends, knowing that He does so for our welfare. To say, "Thy will be done," is the characteristic mark of every child of God. Think of men with such failings and shortcomings as Eli and David. Yet when tragedy came to them each could say, "Let the Lord do as seemeth good unto him." Or think of a righteous man like Job. When the Lord took everything from him — all his wealth, and all his children — and even his wife turned against him, Job said, "The Lord gave, and the Lord hath taken away; blessed be the name of the Lord" (1:21). When his wife told him to renounce God and die he turned to her and said, "Thou speakest as one of the foolish women speaketh. What? Shall we receive good at the hand of God, and shall we not receive evil" (2:10)?

This petition also sets the scope and the frame for all our prayers. Everything that we ask must be within the will of God. We must learn to ask only what is the will of God for us. We must learn to bless the acts of His providence. We reach the heart of all prayer when we learn to say, "Not my will but thy will be done." We must learn to pray as Richard Baxter prayed, "Lord, what Thou wilt, when Thou wilt, where Thou wilt."

A — Petition
B — Pattern

Let us consider now the pattern or the standard for the will of God. The full petition is, "Thy will be done, as in heaven, so on earth." Heaven of course is the place of God's throne, and the place where God's will is done perfectly. The will of God in heaven is done by His angels, and the prayer, "Thy will be done in earth, as it is in heaven," reminds us of the obedience of the angels. Psalm 103 describes the perfect obedience to the will of God in heaven. "The Lord hath prepared his throne in the heavens; and his kingdom ruleth over all. Bless the Lord, ye his angels, that excel in strength, that do his commandments, hearkening unto the voice of his word" (vv. 19-20).

The will of God in heaven is done perfectly and completely, (1) therefore we must learn to do all that God asks of us. We cannot pick and choose which of His commandments we will keep. The person who allows himself some latitude in keeping God's commandments and exempts himself from even one commandment, does not really do God's will at all. He does his own will. It is not until we see that we must completely surrender ourselves, both in our obedience and in our acceptance of the will of God, that we can be said truly to be His children.

This pattern also shows that we must do His will voluntarily. (2) We must not be driven like slaves and yield grudging obedience to God. We must yield ourselves in a cheerful, voluntary obedience to Him, as children of a father. We are not asked to accept the will of God blindly, or to say in mere resignation, "Thy will be done." We must learn to see purpose in God's will and we must learn to trust Him for His goodness.

We must do His will instantly. (3) The angels in heaven are God's ministers who stand ready to serve Him and who instantly carry out every wish and every command of God. When Zacharias, the father of John the Baptist, showed some hesitation to accept the announcement from heaven that he would have a son in his old age, the angel said, "I am Gabriel, that stand in the presence of God; and I was sent to speak unto thee, and to bring thee these good tidings" (Luke 1:19, ASV). Here is an incident that teaches us that the servants of God in heaven are not accustomed to such halting, half-hearted acceptance of God's will and of His Word as we so often give Him here on earth. As we pray, "Thy will be done," let us learn instantly to obey Him and to accept His Word and His will for us without murmuring and without rebellion. /The will of God in heaven is done joyfully. The angels praise God night and day; they delight to do His will. There are some Christian people who have had reverses, disappointments, and trials, and they bear them with some measure of faith and acceptance of the will of God. But they do it in a most mournful, tearful manner. That is not the way that God's will is done in heaven. His servants joyfully obey Him and serve Him. Job did not murmur and say, "All these trials have come upon me, it breaks my heart. I must accept God's will but I don't see why God is so severe with me." Job said, "The Lord gave, the Lord hath taken away, blessed be the name of the Lord."

Perhaps you are thinking, "This is impossible. We are frail human beings; how can we do God's will perfectly, immediately, and joyfully as the angels in heaven obey His will?" /Let me remind you of two things. First, this is a standard, or a pattern. The pattern which God has given us is perfect. In heaven there is perfect obedience to God's will. No pattern would be any good if it were not perfect, in fact the only kind of pattern God could give us is a perfect pattern. It is true that we fall short of it. It is true that none of us completely and perfectly obeys God's will. Even brave and patient Job, who had such marvelous submission to the will of God that he could say, "Blessed be the name of the Lord," when tragedy first struck, later in his life cursed God and asked that he might die. The pattern is perfect and we must make it our goal; we must always aim for God's standard.

The second thing I would like to remind you of is that God's will was once done perfectly upon this earth. In the life and the work of Jesus Christ there was perfect obedience to the will of God. Jesus gave us a perfect example of active obedience in

doing God's will, and passive obedience in accepting and sub-
mitting to the will of God. If you look at the life of Jesus you
will observe that He set the will of God always before Him.
Jesus came to earth to do God's will. He said to His disciples,
"My meat is to do the will of him that sent me, and to finish
his work" (John 4:34). The writer of the letter to the Hebrews,
reviewing the perfect life and obedience of the Son of God, declared that the purpose of it was found in these words, "Lo, I am
come to do thy will, O God" (10:7, ASV). In this the writer of the
letter to the Hebrews shows us that the perfect obedience of the
Son to the Father is our salvation, "By which will we have been
sanctified through the offering of the body of Jesus Christ once
for all" (10:10, ASV).

The Lord Jesus Christ also set the perfect example of obedience in submission to the will of God. In Gethsemane with the
cross before Him, the perfect Man, Jesus, young in years (He
was only thirty-three), looked at that shameful cross and knew
that it meant accepting the guilt and stain of sin. He shrank
from it, and prayed, "Father, if it be possible, let this cup pass
from me. Nevertheless, not my will but thy will be done."

In this perfect obedience of Christ we find not only the pattern
of our obedience but also the power of it. In ourselves we can do
nothing, but in Jesus Christ we can do God's will. Christ is not
only our example, He is our Saviour. By His life and His death
on the cross, His obedience to the will of God becomes our
obedience. God accepts it as such. This is the meaning of His
death for our sins. What we could not do He has done for us.
But by His death He has also broken the power that Satan and
sin and death have over us. In Jesus Christ we have the power
to do God's will. To pray, "Thy will be done in earth, as it is in
heaven," is a prayer for such power. It is to ask God to make us
obedient to Him. It is to pray, as the saints of the Old Testament did when they read the law of God, "Incline my heart unto
thy testimonies" (Psalm 119:36). It is to receive the great benediction of the New Testament, "Now the God of peace, that

brought again from the dead our Lord Jesus, that great shepherd of the sheep, through the blood of the everlasting covenant, make you perfect in every good work to do his will" (Heb. 13:20, 21). God grant that this glorious benediction may rest on each one of us.

CHAPTER VI

# THE PRAYER FOR DAILY BREAD
*"Give us this day our daily bread."*
(MATTHEW 6:11)

The fact that Jesus taught us to pray for bread teaches us something about the scope of prayer. The word *bread* in the Lord's Prayer means not only food but stands for all the needs of the body. When we pray for our daily bread we pray for food and clothes, for work and for health; we pray for the preservation of our earthly life. We learn from this that our physical needs are proper subjects for prayer. The Lord's Prayer covers a wide range. Jesus teaches us that we are to pray not only for the salvation of souls, not only for spiritual things, but He teaches us that we are to pray for food, for work, for a good harvest, for industry, for labor, for all things on which the preservation of our life depends. This petition is a general request to God to supply all our needs.

Because this prayer deals with the preservation of our earthly existence, let us consider some of the lessons that it teaches us about our life here on earth.

The first lesson we learn from this fourth petition of the Lord's Prayer is our total <u>dependence</u> on God for the preservation of our life. By asking God to give us our daily bread we show our dependence upon Him for all things. This is very difficult to realize, particularly for those who live in the cities of this modern world. While I was working on this chapter I had to drop it for an hour to go out to buy the weekly groceries. Walking down

49

the aisle of a modern super market stocked from the floor to the rafters with food makes the connection between God and our food seem quite remote. In our industrial, highly mechanized world many have no sense at all of dependence upon God.

This of course does not mean that the modern man is completely secure in the modern world. In fact he is often most insecure. This is because security and contentment can come only from the knowledge of God and our dependence on Him. The idea of our dependence on God is being revived now in many ways. Some restaurants now have prayer cards on their tables to encourage their patrons to ask a blessing upon their food. I for one have been happy to see them on the tables for it gives me some assurance that when I bow my head in a restaurant to ask God's blessing on the food, the waitress will not come to ask me what is wrong with the soup. These cards are part of a movement to bring America to a deeper recognition of God. By encouraging people to ask God to bless their food and to thank God for it, those who are backing this movement for prayer in restaurants hope to teach men and women their dependence upon God.

Such an emphasis is surely needed. We have shamefully neglected God in our daily life. There has been a practical denial of the power of God in our day. Many act as if God had nothing to do with our daily existence, with our bread and butter. Many who have continued to pray the Lord's Prayer do so only as a form, for even though they pray, "Give us this day our daily bread," they never act as if their bread actually came from God. We must understand therefore that the prayer for daily bread is centered in the teaching of the Bible about the providence of God. This is the knowledge of God we need.

There are some who blame our ignorance of the providence of God on the mechanization of our modern life. They say it is modern industry and business and living in big cities which makes it difficult to think of God as the source of all life. They contend that our modern industrial life has made God seem very remote. I think we may agree that it is not always easy in a modern industrial city to see the relation between our food and God who rules heaven and earth, but the industrialization of our modern life is not the real explanation for our neglect of God. Our failure to recognize our dependence on God arises from the way modern thought has looked at the universe and man's life in it. Through the teaching of naturalism, positivism, and naturalistic evolution, modern man has lost sight of two fundamental facts about God. The first is that God is the almighty Creator and Sustainer of life, and the second is the fact of God's personal love and care for every one of His creatures.

The greatest need for our time is a knowledge of the teaching of the Bible about the nature of God and His relation to our life. Psalm 104 declares, "He causeth the grass to grow for the cattle, and herb for the service of man: that he may bring forth food out of the earth" (v. 14). Not only man but all nature is dependent upon God for life. "The young lions roar after their prey, and seek their meat from God" (Psalm 104:21). Let us learn to exalt God and to exclaim, "O Lord, how manifold are thy works! In wisdom hast thou made them all: The earth is full of thy riches . . . These wait all upon thee; that thou mayest give them their meat in due season" (Psalm 104:24, 27). The Bible not only teaches the power of God, but also reveals the goodness of God. "For the Lord God is a sun and shield; The Lord will give grace and glory; No good thing will he withhold from them that walk uprightly" (Psalm 84:11). "He careth for thee" is a characteristic message of the Bible.

The teaching of the Bible on the providence of God is well summed up in one of our Church catechisms. In explaining the first article of the Apostles' Creed, the question is asked, "What do you believe when you say: I believe in God the Father Almighty, Maker of Heaven and Earth?" "That the eternal Father of our Lord Jesus Christ, who of nothing made heaven and earth, with all that in them is, who likewise upholds and governs the same by His eternal counsel and providence, is for the sake of

Christ His Son my God and my Father, in whom I so trust as to have no doubt that He will provide me with all things necessary for body and soul; and further, that whatever evil He sends upon me in this vale of tears, He will turn to my good; for He is able to do it, being Almighty God, and willing also, being a faithful Father" (Heidelberg Catechism, Lord's Day 9).

The second lesson we learn from this petition is that we must trust God for all things. This is implied in the words *this day* and *daily*. "Give us this day our daily bread" is a prayer asking God for bread for each day on the day. We pray for our needs for one day at a time. Jesus teaches us that we are not to ask for a month's supply, we are not to ask for security for a year or a lifetime, or to ask God for an inheritance. We are to pray only for bread for each day. This of course does not mean that prayer excludes foresight, or work, or thrift on the part of man. The teachings of Jesus, as well as many other parts of the Bible, make it clear that we are to work for our bread and that we are to make proper provision for the future. When some zealous but misguided members of the first church of Christ in Thessalonica quit working, and spent all their time looking for the Lord to return, Paul bluntly laid down the dictum, "If a man will not work let him not eat." Let us understand therefore that reliance on God does not exclude human foresight, provision, and daily work. This prayer teaches us to practice the admonition of the apostle Peter, "Casting all your anxiety upon him, because he careth for you" (I Peter 5:7, ASV).

The fourth petition of the Lord's Prayer teaches us that we must not rely on any material thing such as a bank account, a guaranteed income, an inheritance, or any other material thing for our security. This prayer teaches us that we must trust God alone for our security in the preservation of our life. We must not look upon anything material as a guarantee of our survival; we must believe that God will preserve our lives.

The reason we are to pray for bread for one day at a time is to teach us to trust God for our food and all things necessary for our life. When God fed Israel in the wilderness, He sustained them by His direct power for forty years. He gave them water, meat and bread, but He gave them the bread one day at a time. Every morning the manna came and Israel was instructed to gather enough for one day only. In the wilderness God was teaching His ancient people the same lesson that He intends His people to learn today, that we are to trust Him, and Him only to supply our needs. One of the most beautiful comments written on this petition is by John Wesley. He says that Jesus teaches us to say " 'This day'; For we are to take no thought for the morrow. For this very end has our wise Creator divided life into these little portions of time, so clearly separated from each other; that we might look on every day as a fresh gift of God, another life, which we may devote to His glory; and that every evening may be as the close of life, beyond which we are to see nothing but eternity."

To put our trust in God for our needs is the only cure for worry. As a pastor I have observed that people who have money are often inclined to worry more for their future needs than people who do not have money. I have known men with thousands of dollars in securities and investments to worry about what would happen to them in the years to come. The reason for this is that when we begin to acquire money and property we are tempted to put our trust in money for our security. Jesus said, "Be not therefore anxious, saying, What shall we eat? or, What shall we drink? or, Wherewithal shall we be clothed? For after all these things do the Gentiles seek; for your heavenly Father knoweth that ye have need of all these things" (Matt. 6:31, 32, ASV). When Jesus said, "After all these things do the Gentiles seek," He did not mean that they merely seek material things. What the Gentile, or pagan, seeks is security in material things. The man who does not know God puts his trust for his future provision in money, bonds, property, or anything that is material or tangible. The Christian, on the other hand, must put his trust in God alone for his existence and for his bodily needs, trusting and believing that God will provide all that he needs. This is the reliance on God that we are taught in the Lord's Prayer when Jesus said, "After this manner therefore pray ye: Our Father who art in heaven . . . give us this day our daily bread."

③ The third lesson we learn from this petition is that we must seek moderation in material things. We must learn to be content with plain living. We are taught to pray for bread, not for luxury and extravagance. This does not mean that God promises only enough for mere survival. God does not always limit us to the bare necessities of life. He is a God who delights in abundance. He has made abundant provision for all His creatures. The prayer for bread, however, warns us not to become entangled in the things of this world. A Christian must not set his heart on material things and he must not make his treasure of them. The prayer for bread reminds us that man's life does not consist in the abundance of the things which he possesses. The prayer for bread is in the same vein as that great prayer of an Old Testament child of God, "Give me neither poverty nor riches; Feed me with the food convenient for me" (Prov. 30:8). As we pray for our daily bread let us learn to practice Paul's admonition, "But godliness with contentment is great gain. For we brought nothing into this world, and it is certain we can carry nothing out. And having food and raiment let us be therewith content. But they that will be rich fall into temptation . . . and into many foolish and hurtful lusts, which drown men in destruction and perdition" (I Tim. 6:6–9). "Brown bread and the Gospel is good fare," says an old Gospel writer.

 The fourth lesson we learn from this petition is that we must share the bread God gives us with others. It is not "my" bread, but "our" bread. Here is the social consciousness of the New Testament. The Lord's Prayer teaches each one of us to identify ourselves with our brethren. The nearer we are to Christ, and the more we are filled with the Holy Spirit, the more we will see our responsibility for others, and the more we will desire to share what we have with others. In the early days when the Holy Spirit was poured out upon the church at Pentecost, "all that believed were together, and had all things common" (Acts 2:44). There are some who have said that the practice of community of goods in the New Testament Church was too idealistic for this hard and real world. Remember, however, that Peter, John and Paul, and all the apostles and leaders in the New Testament Church continually insisted that those who were in Jesus Christ should share what they had with others and should be responsible for their brother's needs.

Every book of the New Testament lays upon us a social consciousness and responsibility. John said, "But whoso hath the world's goods, and beholdeth his brother in need, and shutteth up his compassion from him, how doth the love of God abide in him? My little children, let us not love in word, neither with the tongue; but in deed and truth" (I John 3:17, 18, ASV). My friend, have you read lately such passages of the New Testament? Have you read the stern words of James denouncing those who spend everything they have upon themselves, and warning against living in luxury and pleasure on this earth while men are dying of hunger, and suffering from cold and privation (James 5:16)? Every time we as Christian people pray to God for bread, we ask Him for "our" bread. He has given you enough for yourself and for others. Don't spend the surplus; use it for others. Let us learn to love not in word and deed only, but in truth. The next time you pray the prayer our Lord taught us, and you come to the line, "Give us this day our daily bread," think not of your own bread, or your own need only. Think of the millions who have no bread and pray and give that they too may have bread.

# CHAPTER VII

# THE PRAYER FOR FORGIVENESS

*"And forgive us our debts, as we forgive our debtors."*
(MATTHEW 6:12)

An editorial in a recent issue of one of America's leading religious journals points to an amazing deficiency in contemporary preaching. This analysis of modern preaching says that the average sermon is so concerned with telling men how to live, that there is little or no room for the question of prior importance, "How to die."

No man is prepared to die until his sins are forgiven and he is reconciled to God. This is a fundamental fact of our existence and the message of the Gospel of Jesus Christ is that our sins can be forgiven, that God is ready to forgive us and to receive us through faith in His Son Jesus Christ.

In making an analysis of preaching, however, we must be careful not to force the distinction in preaching as preparation for living or preparation for dying. While it is true that no man is ready to die unless his sins are pardoned, it is equally true that no man is ready to live or can really begin to live until his sins are forgiven and he is in fellowship with God. One reason for the sense of insecurity and the tensions in the life of the modern man is that he does not know God and he does not have the peace of God. Peace and hope come into the human heart only through faith in Jesus Christ.

We now come to this question of the forgiveness of sin as we consider the fifth petition in the Lord's Prayer. It may be well to point out again that the six petitions of the Lord's Prayer cover all our basic needs. In the previous chapter we studied the petition, "Give us this day our daily bread," and we observed how this one petition covers all of man's physical needs. In this chapter we observe how Jesus taught us to pray for our spiritual need when He said, "After this manner therefore pray ye . . . forgive us our debts, as we forgive our debtors."

For a full understanding of the meaning of this petition let us look first of all at the description of sin given in the Lord's Prayer. We learn here that sin is a debt. There are several words in the Bible to describe what sin is but all of them emphasize the fact that sin is an offense against God. Jesus described man's sin as a debt that man is unable to pay: "There was a certain creditor which had two debtors . . . and when they had nothing to pay, he frankly forgave them both" (Luke 7:41, 42). This is intended to teach us that we are utterly insolvent. We have wasted our substance, we have nothing to pay.

When Jesus speaks of sin as a debt, He means that sin incurs an account which must be settled. You cannot escape a debt. If you owe someone a considerable sum of money you may be glad to forget it, but your creditor will not. Just as there are people who have careless and easy-going attitudes toward money, so there are millions who have careless and easy-going attitudes toward sin. We need to hear again the plain teaching of the Bible that sin incurs guilt and punishment. We need to face the direct questions of the Bible: "And thinkest thou this, O man, that judgest them which do such things, and doest the same, that thou shalt escape the judgment of God" (Rom. 2:3)? "Or despisest thou the riches of his goodness and forbearance and longsuffering, not knowing that the goodness of God leadeth thee to repentance?" God is righteous and holy, and there is no other way that He can deal with sin, than either to forgive it freely or to let the penalty of sin come upon all those who are disobedient and ignore His grace and mercy. It is for this reason that Jesus taught us to pray, "Our Father who art in heaven . . . forgive us our debts."

I am well aware that there are other views of the nature of sin. Many modern theologians and psychologists speak of sin as mere weakness, or lack of adjustment, or immaturity, but for all who hold a view of sin other than the one that is given in the Lord's Prayer, I ask, What is your authority? That sin is a debt, and that sin incurs guilt and punishment is the view of sin taught by Jesus, and the apostles.

A debt must be settled with the man to whom it is owed. Suppose you owe a man $10,000 and you are not able to pay it. You begin to worry about your debt. You may even go to your friends and ask their opinion of it. They may say to you they think your creditor will be lenient, or that he will give you more time, or that he will reduce the rate of interest, but their opinions really count for nothing. The only man who has any authority to make any decision about the debt is the man to whom it is owed. This is exactly what Jesus meant to teach us about our relation to God, and for this reason He so frequently compared sin to a debt. Because of our sins we are under obligation to God and only God can deal with the penalty of sin. It matters not therefore what your friends may think about you, how good they think you are; the only thing that matters is what God thinks about you. Therefore Jesus directs you to God for the forgiveness of your sins. Only God can show us mercy. Only God can forgive us. For that reason Jesus said, "After this manner therefore pray ye: Our Father who art in heaven . . . forgive us our debts as we forgive our debtors."

The second lesson we learn from this petition is that God freely forgives our sins. Jesus taught us to come to God and ask for the forgiveness of our sins because God does forgive sin. Again and again Jesus said to the people, "Your sins are forgiven." The Word of God promises us free forgiveness for all our sins. It declares, there is forgiveness with God. Have you ever thought of the wonder of forgiveness? It is the greatest of all miracles. There have been men who have rejected Christianity because they said that forgiveness is impossible. Forgiveness is possible, but only for God and only because He is infinite in wisdom, power and grace.

Forgiveness is the greatest of all God's gifts because of what it does. It does two things. First, in forgiveness God cancels the penalty and the eternal punishment of sin. The eternal moral law is, "The soul that sinneth it shall die." "The wages of sin is death." When God forgives our sins He does not cancel that law but He takes the curse and the penalty of sin upon Himself, in Jesus Christ on the cross, so that the curse and the penalty do not fall upon us. This is the message of the Gospel. Paul reminds the church of that pure Gospel message when he writes to the Corinthians, "For I delivered unto you first of all that which I also received, how that Christ died for our sins according to the scriptures" (I Cor. 15:3). In his letter to the Galatians he defines this more exactly when he says, "Christ hath redeemed us from the curse of the law, being made a curse for us: for it is written, Cursed is every one that hangeth on a tree" (3:13).  The second part of forgiveness is that God restores us to fellowship and favor with Himself. "If we confess our sins, he is faithful and just to forgive us our sins, and to cleanse us from all unrighteousness" (I John 1:9). Forgiveness is not merely removal of the penalty. It is a positive act in the restoration of the sinner to fellowship and favor with God forever.

There are some who have wondered why the Lord taught us to pray for bread first, and why the petition for forgiveness comes after the cry for bread. The reason is obvious when we consider that forgiveness is the greatest of all God's gifts. The highest and best gift comes last. Though we have all things, if we have not the forgiveness of our sins we have nothing. This is what David meant when he said, "Thy lovingkindness is better than life" (Psalm 63:3). What is food or bodily nourishment without the hope of heaven? We are rich when we are reconciled to God. Forgiveness of sin is better than silver or gold, or stocks or bonds, or a bank account, or any other treasure that this world can offer. If we have peace with God we have all things; if we are not at peace with God and do not have our sins forgiven we have nothing. "What shall it profit a man if he gain the whole world and lose his own soul?"

In spite of this there are many who still cry only for bread. Even some church members show by their actions that they value money more than they do the mercy and the grace of God. These days when we make so much of money and all material things we need to hear again the warning of Jesus delivered to the milling crowds of Galilee who sought only material bread. Jesus rebuked them and said, "Verily, verily, I say unto you, Ye seek me, not because ye saw signs, but because ye ate of the loaves and were filled. Work not for the food which perisheth but for the food which abideth unto eternal life, which the Son of man shall give unto you: for him the Father, even God, hath sealed" (John 6:26, 27, ASV).

Let us consider next how we must pray to God for forgiveness. Jesus said, "After this manner therefore pray ye: Our Father who art in heaven . . . forgive us our debts." How must we confess our sins to God?

First, confession of sin must be personal. Jesus said that we must come to God saying, "Forgive us *our* debts." A true confession of sin is a personal acknowledgment of guilt. This is not easy, for we are naturally inclined to be evasive about our sins. "Not my sin," said Adam, the first man, "but the woman's." "Not my sin," said the woman, "but the serpent's." And so today we who are sinful and guilty before God still hesitate to acknowledge our own sins. Sin is a shameful, filthy thing and we are inclined to cover it up, to hide it. The Bible teaches that the only way to acquittal before God is for each person to make a frank, personal acknowledgment of sin to God, who will hear us and forgive us. "I acknowledged my sin unto thee, and mine iniquity have I not hid. I said, I will confess my transgressions unto the Lord; And thou forgavest the iniquity of my sin" (Psalm 32:5).

If you want peace in your soul, if you want your sin covered by the blood of the Lord Jesus Christ, do what David did—frankly acknowledge your sin and guilt to God and peace will come into your soul. Until we are willing to say that our sins are only ours, that they are wholly and totally ours, we have not made a genuine confession of sin.

Second, the confession of sin must be specific. Most of our prayers for forgiveness and most of our confession of sins are too general. There are many people who have never made any other confession of sin than to pray, "Lord, forgive our many sins." The way to peace and to the assurance of pardon is to name our sins before God. If you have lied, confess your lies to God. If you are guilty of adultery, name it before the Lord. Whatever it may be — an evil, sinful thought, jealousy, lust, envy, pride — name the sin to God when you ask Him to forgive it.

Third, confession of sin must be sincere. We often hear it said that if we are sorry for our sins, God will forgive us. This is true if we rightly understand what sorrow for sin is. To be sorry for sin is more than a mere repetition of words, or an emotion. It is more than to be sorry for the consequences of sin. An old writer says, "A man may be sorry, not that he has sinned, but that it is not lawful to sin." Genuine sorrow of heart has two marks: a real hatred of sin because it is an offense against God our heavenly Father, and a sincere purpose to forsake our sin. All true sorrow for sin must have these two marks. We must hate sin and we must sincerely determine to forsake it. The order of the Bible is, Confess and forsake your sin (Prov. 28:13).

This does not mean that we cannot come back to God after our failures. We repeatedly fall into sin but each new confession of sin must have a sincere resolve to forsake the sin. There must be a constant forsaking of sin in our lives. If we thus genuinely confess our sin to God, and if we sincerely resolve to forsake it, God will give us the strength to overcome it. In the forgiveness of sin there is implied the victory over sin. When we sing and praise God for the power of the blood of the Lord Jesus, we mean not only power to obtain pardon from God but we mean that there is power in the blood to win victory over sin. You too can conquer sin. You can break that habit. You can forsake your sin by faith in Jesus Christ. Whatever sin you are struggling with now, whatever evil temptation faces you, remember that some of God's children have already conquered that same sin in Christ, and what others have done you too can do through the Lord, who forgives you.

Fourth, we must come to God with confidence that He will forgive us. If we come to Him in true repentance and faith we must expect that He will forgive us. It is His nature to forgive us. God is love, God is gracious and merciful. His mercy is infinite. The Bible speaks of the dimensions of the love and the mercy of God. It speaks of the height and the depth, the length and the breadth of the love of God. The infinite mercy of God is the ground for our forgiveness. Moreover, we have confidence that He will forgive us because He has demonstrated His love in Jesus Christ. "For God so loved the world that he gave his only begotten Son, that whosoever believeth on him should not perish, but have eternal life" (John 3:16, ASV). Even if you have sinned many times, if you have multiplied your sins, if you truly grieve over them and come to God in repentance and faith, He will multiply His pardon. "Let the wicked forsake his way and the unrighteous man his thoughts . . . and he will have mercy upon him; and to our God, for he will abundantly pardon" (Isa. 55:7).

Let us consider, finally, the obligation of a forgiven man. "Forgive us our debts, as we forgive our debtors" is the full petition. Because God has freely forgiven us we must also forgive those who have offended us. Forgiveness means that you cannot harbor in your heart resentment, hatred, or enmity against such a person. This is a solemn obligation laid upon you by the Lord. This is the only petition in the Lord's Prayer to which Jesus added an interpretative comment. At the conclusion of the prayer Jesus added, "For if ye forgive men their trespasses, your heavenly Father will also forgive you. But if ye forgive not men their trespasses, neither will your Father forgive your trespasses." (Matthew 6:14, 15). Nothing shows more clearly the necessity laid upon the Christian to forgive all offenses committed against him.

Some years ago I tried to reconcile two men who had a quarrel about business, that resulted in deep personal resentment against each other. They were both members of the same church and they had been partners in the same business. Their quarrel grew to such proportions that it was necessary that something be done. I visited both parties. After some time one man agreed to a reconciliation. I then went to the second man but he was adamant. He refused to yield. He expressed hatred for the first man. I used every argument I could from the Word of God to show that he could not hate and be a Christian, but nothing moved him. The man had stopped attending the services of the church, so I asked him, "Do you still pray?" "Oh, yes," he said. "I am not a heathen. I pray in my home." I said, "Do you pray the Lord's Prayer?" "Yes," he said, "we use the Lord's Prayer daily." I said to him, "What do you do with this line, 'Forgive us our debts as we forgive our debtors'?" There was a long pause. I prayed that God would melt his heart, but finally he spoke, his eyes flashed with anger as he said, "From now on I will leave that part out." If that shocks you, let me remind you that he was at least consistent. Unless you forgive you had better not pray the Lord's Prayer. For to say, "Forgive us our debts as we forgive our debtors" and to refuse to forgive is to make the Lord's Prayer a curse instead of a blessing. Listen again to the words of Jesus. "For if ye forgive men their trespasses, your heavenly Father will also forgive you. But if ye forgive not men their trespasses, neither will your Father forgive your trespasses" (Matt. 6:14, 15).

# CHAPTER VIII

# THE PRAYER FOR DELIVERANCE FROM EVIL

*"And lead us not into temptation,*
*but deliver us from evil."*

(MATTHEW 6:13a)

Some years ago a college professor came to me and said, "I hate to admit this, but I have prayed the Lord's Prayer all my life and have never understood the meaning of this part: 'Lead us not into temptation.' Do we have to ask God not to lead us into temptation?" The professor's question points out a difficulty many people have in understanding this part of the Lord's Prayer. To them this petition seems to imply that God leads us into temptation. Those who know the Bible know of course that this is impossible, for the book of James says, "Let no man say when he is tempted, I am tempted of God; for God cannot be tempted with evil, neither tempteth he any man" (1:13).

Failure to understand this petition of the Lord's Prayer is due primarily to two causes. One reason for the misunderstanding lies in the way the petitions are sometimes divided. If we make the first part—"Lead us not into temptation"—a separate and distinct petition, we run into problems, but if we take the whole sentence—"Lead us not into temptation, but deliver us from evil"—as one petition there is no difficulty at all, for we see that this is a prayer to God for deliverance from temptation and evil.

A second reason many do not understand the full meaning of this petition is due to a failure to make a distinction in the kinds of temptation. In the early days of the English language the word *temptation* had a broader usage than it does now. It was used to express two distinct ideas: enticement to sin, and trials or afflictions. Today in the English language we use two words for these ideas. We use the word *temptation* in the evil sense, as enticement to sin, and we use the word *trial* to represent the idea of testing one's faith under affliction. This distinction is found in the book of James. James says in the first chapter of his letter, "My brethren, count it all joy when ye fall into divers temptations; knowing this that the trying of your faith worketh patience" (1:2, 3). It is obvious that he is using the word *temptation* here in the sense of trial, or affliction, and the words he uses is so translated in the R.S.V. On the other hand in the same chapter James says, "Let no man say when he is tempted, I am tempted of God; for God cannot be tempted with evil, neither tempteth he any man" (1:13). Here the word *temptation* is used for enticement to sin.

The word *temptation* in the Lord's Prayer means primarily temptation to sin. It is not a prayer to God to keep us out of trials and difficulties but a prayer to deliver us from sin and evil. The Bible makes it quite clear that God sends affliction upon us and that He does it for our good. It was God who tempted, or tried, Abraham in order to test his faith. Jesus said, "Blessed are they which are persecuted for righteousness' sake: for theirs is the kingdom of heaven. Blessed are ye, when men shall revile you, and persecute you, and shall say all manner of evil against you falsely, for my sake. Rejoice, and be exceeding glad: for great is your reward in heaven: for so persecuted they the prophets which were before you" (Matt. 5:10-12). James says, "Count it all joy, brethren, when you meet various trials" or again, "Blessed is the man who endures trials for when he has stood the test, he will receive the crown of life, which God has promised to those who love him" (1:12, R.S.V.).

God knows that we need such trials and afflictions for spiritual growth. In the letter to the Hebrews we are taught that it is a mark of the special favor of God when chastening comes. "Whom the Lord loveth he chasteneth." Trials and afflictions are a mark of sonship. God afflicts us for our benefit so that we may be partakers of holiness (Heb. 12:10). God sends us trials because He knows how much we need them. There is an old adage which reveals human nature as it is. We often say, "He couldn't stand prosperity." This teaches us that we need adversity. For the development of strength in character we need some measure of adversity.

It is apparent therefore that this is not a prayer in which we ask God to exempt us from trials. This is a prayer to be kept from enticement to sin. It is a prayer to be delivered out of all sin and evil. Augustine paraphrased it as follows: "Suffer us not to be led into." A. T. Robertson, one of the greatest New Testament scholars of this century, speaking of the first words of this petition, says, "This is a 'permissive imperative.' It means 'Do not allow us to be led into temptation,' that is, into enticement to sin." Calvin summarizes the meaning of this petition with his usual clarity, "Our petition, therefore is, that we may not fall under temptation; that being thus taken under God's charge and protection, we may remain invincible by sin, death, the gates of hell, and the whole power of the devil; in other words, be delivered from evil."

Having considered the meaning of this part of the Lord's Prayer, let us observe next what we pray for in this petition. We ask God for three things. We pray first of all that we may not be lured into sin. Remember, God does not entice us to evil. In this prayer we ask God not to permit others to lure us into evil. This prayer exposes the three great enemies of our spiritual life: the world, the flesh, and the devil. Satan is the supreme enemy of God and our souls, and he is the tempter, the evil mind and personality behind all the forces that would draw us away from God and eternal life. The flesh is our own sinful nature which is corrupted by sin and inclined to yield to evil. The world is life organized apart from God, seeking satisfaction and contentment in material things. This prayer therefore is a petition to God that He will not permit any of these enemies of our souls to draw us away from Him and from eternal life. It is a prayer that we may not be caught off guard and fall into temptation and sin.

(2) Secondly, this is a petition that we may not <u>yield</u> to temptation. In offering this prayer we acknowledge our own weakness and the power of our enemies. It is a recognition of our complete dependence upon God. There is a very important relation between the fifth petition and the sixth petition of the Lord's Prayer. To pray, "Forgive us our debts, as we forgive our debtors" is to pray for pardon from sin. But to pray, "Lead us not into temptation, but deliver us from evil" is to pray for a positive spiritual character so that we may resist all evil. The forgiven man knows the danger of sin. He knows what sin can do, he knows its awful power and terrible penalty, and therefore he prays earnestly to be delivered from the power and from all the evil, destructive force in sin.

(3) In the third place this is a prayer for <u>complete victory</u> over sin and evil. We ask God for power to overcome sin and temptation. This is a prayer for sanctification and holiness. The meaning is: "Since we are so weak in ourselves that we cannot stand a moment, while our deadly enemies—the devil, the world, and our own flesh assail us without ceasing, be pleased to preserve and strengthen us by the power of Thy Holy Spirit, that we make firm stand against them, and not sink in this spiritual war, until we come off at last with complete victory" (Heidelberg Catechism, Lord's Day 52). It is a mark of true repentance to long for such victory. We are not truly repentant if we desire only pardon from sin; the true penitent longs for victory over temptation and sin.

It is apparent therefore that if we <u>sincerely</u> pray, "Lead us not into temptation, but deliver us from evil," we must ourselves <u>be on guard</u> against every form of sin and evil. Jesus said, "<u>Watch and pray that ye enter not into temptation</u>." Watching and praying go together. We must therefore guard against the very

beginning of sin. We must guard our thoughts and our minds ①
so that we may not be led into the desire to sin. The Bible
teaches us how temptation works and if we do not know our
own hearts the Bible will show us what our hearts are like. The
Bible says, "But each man is tempted, when he is drawn away by
his own lust and enticed. Then the lust, when it hath conceived,
beareth sin; and the sin, when it is fullgrown, bringeth forth
death" (James 1:14, 15, ASV). The best place to make a stand
against temptation is at the very beginning. Guard your mind,
watch your thoughts.

We must avoid all <u>unnecessary risks.</u> Every person has his own ②
weakness, and we know what these weaknesses are and what our
particular nature is. Clarence Macartney says, "<u>Every soul
has its own ladder down to hell.</u>" There may be a <u>book</u> another
person can read, but you can't read that book without being
tempted. There are <u>pictures</u> that you cannot look at. There
is <u>company</u> that you cannot keep. There are forms of commercial
amusements that you must leave alone lest you lose your soul.
As you pray to God that you may not be led into temptation, you
must not unnecessarily expose yourself to danger and to evil.

There ought also to be on our part a <u>positive resistance to evil.</u> ③
Martin Luther was not only a great theologian and a great
preacher; he was also a great Christian. Few men have been
tempted as he was, not only in his own person, but in his great
struggle against tyranny. Every one has heard the story of how
Luther in one period of temptation in the castle of Wartburg
stood up from his desk, took his ink stand and hurled it at the
devil. This is the kind of positive resistance to sin that we all
need. The Bible says, "<u>Resist the devil and he will flee from you.</u>"
One of the greatest tragedies of our time is the passive surrender
countless thousands have made to sin and evil. They quietly
give up the struggle. This need not be. God gives us the strength
to fight against all sin and all evil.

The prayer "Lead us not into temptation, but deliver us from
evil" is not only a cry to God for help and for deliverance, but it

holds out the promise of victory. If you are tempted to surrender and give up the struggle, hear this message of encouragement from the Word of God. Victory is possible for you. "Wherefore lift up the hands which hang down, and the feeble knees" (Heb. 12:12). This victory is possible in Jesus Christ. Put your trust in Jesus, confess Him as your Saviour. If you are thus united to Him by faith you will find a power, not your own, fighting for you. You will find Him standing beside you and giving you the victory. You will learn to say with Paul and millions of believers, "I can do all things in Christ who strengthens me." You cannot do it alone, the arm of flesh will fail you, but you can do it in Jesus Christ.

In this spiritual warfare God gives you two weapons that will win the victory for you against temptation, sin and evil. The first is the sword of the Spirit, which is the Word of God. Armed with this sword you can conquer the enemy. Obviously, a sword is no good to a person who doesn't know how to use it. A man must be trained in the use of the sword, so that it will become a defensive weapon. The same thing is true of the Scriptures. We must know how to use the Bible if it is to be an effective weapon against sin and evil. In my own life I had to learn how to use the Bible. There were times when temptations overcame me, when the world, the flesh, and the devil all seemed to make their assault at the same time. I would turn to the Bible for deliverance. I paged furiously through it for some text that would ward off the evil one, and all his allurements to sin. It was some time before I learned how to use the Bible as a weapon in time of temptation. The writer of the 119th Psalm said, "Thy word have I laid up in my heart, that I might not sin against thee" (v. 11, ASV). When the Tempter came to Jesus it was with Scripture that Jesus won the victory. Three times over in that momentous struggle Jesus turned to Satan and He said, "But it is written . . . "

The second powerful weapon against temptation and sin is prayer. In *Pilgrim's Progress* Bunyan describes two battles Christian had with Satan. In the first Apollyon attacked Christian in a personal encounter and that fight was won by Christian with the sword of the Spirit, which is the Word of God. In the second battle Christian had to go through the valley of the shadow of death, and then hell loosed its assault upon his soul. Here Christian found that he needed more than his knowledge of Scripture to survive. He needed another weapon. He found it in prayer. Bunyan, by putting two words together from the sixth chapter of Ephesians, called it All-Prayer. It was by persevering, believing prayer that Christian was delivered from the powers of hell, and won the victory over sin and evil.

No matter how many times you have been defeated, no matter how many times you have been tempted to give up the struggle, hear God's promise to you. Victory is possible. God's children have won the victory in every generation, and you too can win this complete victory over all sin. Pray for it! Pray in faith, "Lead us not into temptation, but deliver us from evil," and God will deliver you.